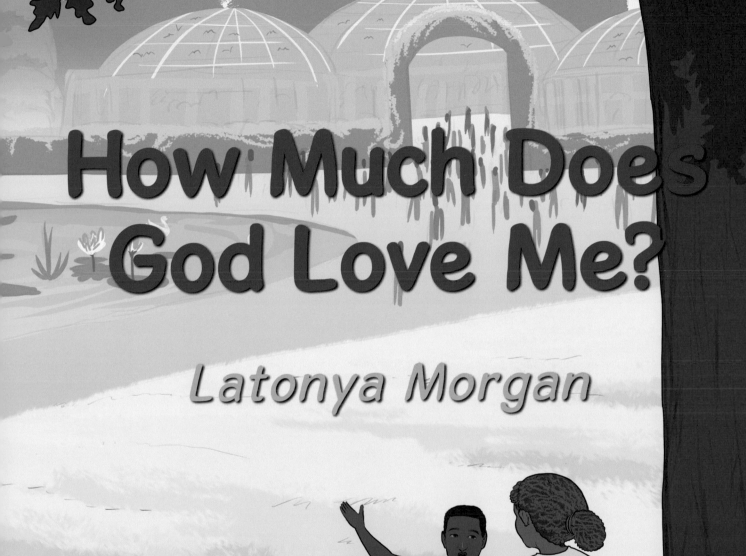

How Much Does God Love Me?

Latonya Morgan

To order additional copies of this book, contact:
Xlibris
1-888-795-4274
www.Xlibris.com
Orders@Xlibris.com

A Note from the Author

It is so important that our children know that God, the father of Jesus Christ, loves them so much. They need to know that whatever they're going through, God is there for them just as He is there for us. It is critical that they know that there is someone greater than their moms, dads, brothers, and sisters who will fight on their behalf.

They must know that God understands and sees things that occur in and around their lives and that He has given them power over their situations. There is no age limit in using godly wisdom and having a relationship with Christ. Children are precious gifts from God, and they need to know that. They are loved beyond comprehension, and it's time to get the word out about that love.

One night as Cameron sat by the living room window, he gazed up at the sky. He sat there with his dad and brother for a while, watching the moon glow. Suddenly he turned and asked his dad, "How much does God love me?"

His dad was taken aback at this question. He paused for a moment, then took Cameron in his arms and pointed to the sky. He asked Cameron, "Do you see all those beautiful stars and that big glowing moon?" Cameron nodded yes. Dad said, "God created the stars and the moon and you, yet He loves you more."

Psalm 8:3–4

[3]When I considered Your heavens, the work of your fingers, The moon and stars, which You have ordained,

[4]What is man that you are mindful of him, and the son of man that you visit him?

The next day Cameron and his family went to the botanical gardens. It was a beautiful day, and they had a picnic under a large oak tree. As Cameron ate quietly, he stared out at the field of flowers and trees. He watched as the pretty butterflies and birds flew around them. Then he asked his mom, "How much does God love me?"

His mom thought for a moment, then answered him, saying, "Do you see the field of flowers and trees that seem to go on forever?" Cameron said yes. Mom then said, "God loves you so much that your beauty shall never fade like the flowers or wither like the trees. That is how much God loves you."

Isaiah 40:6

All flesh is grass, and all its loveliness is like the flowers of the field.

Cameron and his brother, Caden, went to the aquarium with their aunt. They were having so much fun watching the different fishes, big and small. When they came across the whales' tank, Cameron and Caden were amazed at how large the creatures were. Then a familiar question came to Cameron, and he asked his aunt, "How much does God love me?"

Well, his aunt replied, "God loves you and Caden so much that He gave you power over all the fish of the sea, the small and large fish God gave to you two. That's how much God loves you."

Genesis 1:28

And God said to them, have dominion over the fish of the sea, over the birds of the air, and over every living thing that moves on the earth.

The family decided to take a road trip. They sang many songs along the way until Cameron began to get tired. As he began to fall asleep, he noticed an injured animal left on the side of the road, and his heart went out to it because there was no one there to help it. Cameron then asked, "How much does God love me?" He asked no one in particular.

Dad answered, "God loves you so much that he will never leave you when you are hurt, sad, or not feeling well."

Hebrews 13:5

For He Himself has said, I will never leave you nor forsake you.

One afternoon Cameron and Caden were playing with their toys. Cameron was stocking his blocks into a castle, when he noticed Caden playing with his truck. He ran over and snatched it from Caden, who then began to cry. Dad rushed in to see what was going on. Cameron was sent to timeout, and Caden cried himself to sleep.

After a while, Dad called Cameron into the room, and he entered in quietly. He saw nothing wrong in what he had done; after all, it was his toy. He asked his dad, "How much does God love me?"

Dad was glad to answer this question; it was time Cameron learned about sharing. "God loves you so much that He has provided you with many toys, not just so you can play with them, but so you can share with others too, especially your brother."

Cameron paused and thought for a moment. He did have a lot of toys and couldn't possibly play with them all at the same time. And he loved his brother so much that he decided not to just share but to also give Caden his truck. He couldn't wait for his brother to wake up and apologize for being mean.

1 Timothy 6:18

Let them do good, that they be rich in good works ready to give, willing to share.

Caden watched the other children on the playground. He was still too small to play with the big children. He had tried to keep up with them, but they were too fast. Caden was a little sad; there was no one to play with. After a while, he asked a question he'd heard his brother ask many times. "Mommy, how much does God love me?" Caden asked.

His mom saw what was going on and replied, saying, "God loves you so much that He is your friend. God will play with you when no one else will. You're not too small for Him."

Matthew 19:14

But Jesus said, "Let the little children come to me, and do not hinder them, for the kingdom of heaven belongs to such as these.

Caden smiled and jumped down from the bench and said, "Come on, God, let's play on the jungle gym." He swung on the swings and went down the slides. He had forgotten all about the other children. Caden was having so much fun playing with God that he didn't notice the other children as they made their way over to where he was. They watched as he made up awesome games to play. None of the older children had thought of games the way Caden did, and they wanted to play along with him and God.

Psalm 144:15

Happy is that people, that is in such a case: yea, happy is that people, whose God is the Lord.

As Caden played with his new friend, God, he noticed a big child messing with some smaller ones. This big kid made his way around the playground, bullying each child that happened to be in his sight. Caden asked his new friend, "God, how much do you love him?"

Mom overheard this and said, "God loves him so much that He sees the good in that child even though he's acting out."

Romans 3:24

Being justified freely by his grace through the redemption that is in Christ Jesus.

Caden thought for a while, and by then the big kid had made his way over. Caden looked up and smiled. He sure was a big kid. Some time went by before Caden asked if he wanted to play. The big kid looked shocked by the question, so Caden asked again. The big kid answered yes, and they played with toys.

Leviticus 19:18

Thou shalt not avenge, nor bear any grudge against the children of thy people, but thou shalt love thy neighbor as thyself: I am the Lord.

Suddenly Caden asked the kid what his name was. He replied, "My name is Jemal. What's yours?" Caden told him. They played a little bit more before Caden asked Jemal why he was bullying the other children. Jemal was saddened as he answered, "They wouldn't play with me because I'm too big." They had called him names that were hurtful, and in return, Jemal used his bigness to get back at them.

Caden thought for a moment, and then he asked Jemal if he would be his friend. That put a smile on Jemal's face. He was so happy he couldn't speak. So he nodded his head yes. That day Caden had made two friends that didn't care about his size, God and Jemal.

Proverbs 18:24

A man that hath friends must show himself friendly: and there is a friend that sticks closer than a brother.

Printed in the United States
By Bookmasters